To my husband Glenn!

You believed that I could, so I did. Your love and support helped me write the sweetest book about our little camper. We are an effective team my dear... I love you!!

THE ADVENTURES OF

LIL' CUTIE

Hi! My name is Lil' Cutie
and this is my story.

I lived on a beautiful farm out in the country, surrounded by big, open fields. On this farm, there was a beautiful white house where Farmer Henry and his family lived. I loved living on our farm. There were so many animals, and I called them all my friends. You see, I lived in a barn with all of them. I know—a camper? That lived in a barn? That sounds kind of funny, doesn't it?

But it's true. Farmer Henry put me in the barn, because I had an important job. I kept all the horses' saddles and bridles safe and dry. The cozy barn was my home.

There were cows in the barn with me, along
with some horses, a muddy pig named Petunia,
and lots of noisy chickens. It was wonderful
being in that barn.

We all lived there happily for years. But as time went by, I would daydream about being outside. I wanted to feel the sun on my face and the cool rain on my roof.

The months turned into years, and eventually, the farm animals left one by one, and then ... there was just me. My tires were old, rotted, and flat. I was dirty, but worst of all, I was lonely. Nobody ever came out to the barn anymore. Once in a while, I could hear trucks go down the road, or I could hear a plane flying in the sky.

I would remember the excitement of being pulled down the road by Farmer Henry's truck. How I missed those days. I thought I would never get to leave that barn again, but boy was I wrong!

One day, a man named Jake came out to the farm to fix Farmer Henry's tractor. The man asked about the dirty little camper in the barn, and Farmer Henry told him, "If you can get that camper out of this barn, you can have it!"

Jake made a phone call, and an hour later, a tow truck was coming down the driveway! Carefully and slowly, they worked to get me out of the barn. I really didn't think they would be able to get me out, because I was really stuck. But it happened—the next thing I knew, I was outside! I couldn't believe it. The sun was on my face, and it felt incredible!

They were very careful when they put me on the back of the tow truck. I said goodbye to the farm and down the road I went.

My life changed forever that day. I was definitely excited, but I was a little nervous too. I hadn't been out of the barn for years, and now here I was, going down the road. Sometimes, going to new places and trying new things can be a little scary. But I was going to be brave! I couldn't wait to see my new home and travel the roads again!

We drove for just a little while, and then the next thing I knew, we were pulling into a driveway. My new house was out in the country, too, and it was surrounded by trees. I was happy and excited to arrive at my new home.

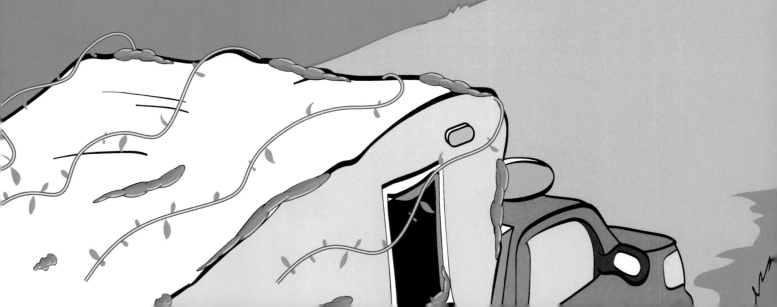

They took me off the tow truck and parked me next to the garage. A pretty woman named Ellie came out of the house, looked at me and giggled. "What is this thing?" Jake smiled at Ellie and then looked at me. "I know," he said, "she's not very pretty right now, but you wait and see. I will clean her up and make her brand new again!"

The first thing Jake did was look me over, and he noticed that I was pretty dirty. Years of dirt and barn dust were caked all over me. It was time for my first bath!

Jake got out the garden hose, a scrub brush, and a big bucket filled with sudsy soap. It took him a long time to get me clean, because I was really dirty! It felt great to be clean again.

After Jake was done, he stood back, stared at me and smiled. His little brown and white camper looked amazing!

Jake worked on me every day after work. His friends would come over and see how much time and work he had put into the camper, but they still laughed. All they could see was an ugly little camper. Jake didn't care that they laughed, because he knew that they would think differently someday.

Jake continued to work on me every chance he had.
I even got new tires on one day! Wow! It was like
having a new pair of shoes. They felt wonderful!

One cool, autumn evening, Jake called Ellie down to the garage. He wanted to show her what he had done to the camper.

He had fixed my outside lights!
My blinkers worked, too. I was
coming to life again, and it felt
wonderful! I hadn't felt this
alive in a long time. My lights
lit up the garage, and Ellie
smiled and clapped her hands
with excitement.

She said I looked adorable, and then she said the most beautiful words I had ever heard. "This is the cutest camper I have ever seen. We are just going to have to name her that. Welcome to the family, Lil' Cutie!"

I loved my new family, and they loved me! Jake continued to work on me almost every day. He made a kitchen, a little bathroom and a place where they could sleep. Jake and Ellie both worked on making me beautiful. They had pretty curtains made, and I even had a cool black and white checkered floor. I was really looking like a new camper!

The months went by quickly, and that spring day seemed to be like every other day, but it wasn't. Something was different about Jake. He asked me if I was ready to go on an adventure.

He said it was time for me to get painted! What? No more brown and white? Jake said that they had chosen something called "vintage blue," and I couldn't wait to see it.

Jake hooked me up to his truck, and down the road we went! He dropped me off at the paint shop, and I was gone for weeks. They worked hard on me. I was covered in tape and plastic most of the time, but it was worth it.

Because when they were finished, I looked like a brand-new camper! When Jake came to pick me up, he saw me and smiled! I was now blue and white, and I sparkled like a new penny! Jake hooked me back up to his truck, and we headed home.

Ellie was waiting in the yard for us, and as we pulled down the driveway, she clapped her hands again! She couldn't believe how beautiful I was. And you know what? I felt beautiful.

Made in the USA
Columbia, SC
30 April 2025

57375902R00018